Vaccy Years

Leon Wing

Published by WingWorldWeb, 2023.

While every precaution has been taken in the preparation of this book, the publisher assumes no responsibility for errors or omissions, or for damages resulting from the use of the information contained herein.

VACCY YEARS

First edition. January 1, 2023.

ISBN: 979-8215142707

Written by Leon Wing.

Also by Leon Wing

Chow Kit Chronicles
Becoming Ah Lan Toh
Boy Man Girl and Back
Orlando Rises
Chushi

Standalone
They Came Stomping : The Remixes
Drawing Sounds
Little Big Lies : Micro Stories
Mixed Signals
Hung
Signs
Kwailo and Other Strange Tales
Vaccy Years

Watch for more at wingsworldweb.tumblr.com.

Table of Contents

About the Chapbook

A mini collection, beginning, naturally, with the first day of the New Year, whichever it was: probably the pandemic year of 2020. It was exacerbated by a long bout of water cuts caused by a factory dumping toxic waste into the river. The rest of the collection : new year resolution, passing of a friend's husband, my escape from damage when I fell backwards down a flight of stairs, angelic presence; another death, this time my cat; lucid dreaming. Lastly, a few haiku.

Image by Maddi Bazzocco from *Unsplash*

1st Day of the New Year

The first day of the New Year
decides that I should walk like an Egyptian,
one foot back, one forward,
dragging myself in a slow march.
I gush, all breathy, like an obscene phone call
from a subterranean cave.
The engine revving like my heart,
I ride shotgun to the A&E, where
I shoot the roof like a pressure cooker in 200 points.
Not an attack of the clones, and
if the points gain higher, rather of the heart.
Nozzles up my nose, I lie with sticky pads all over me,
a clasp over my finger, for vital signs,
"Sharp scratch" and then something sucks my blood.
A reverse viewing on a plastic sheet defines
the sloshing inside my chest.
I am drowning, unless Fluimucil and amlopidine save me.

Vaccer Trilogy

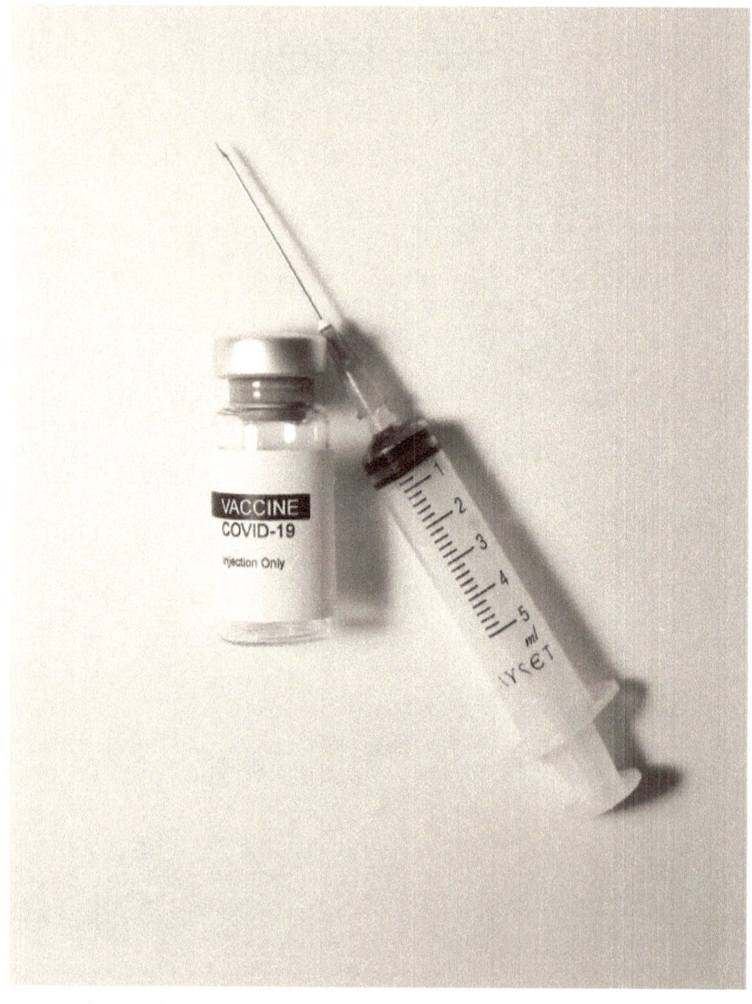

Image by Hakan Nural from *Unsplash*

Haiku: Jab

the world's coming a
part but not for the pub go
er in Manchester

Image by Ant Rozetsky from *Unsplash*

Riding the Bus to WTC Vaccination Center

I wish I was a flaming homo, he muttered. Really I do, you get it?
I butted my head against the window, must I listen to this? He
turned around

and creased his eyes. His hair, still wet from the bukkake,
was black as a ho from Chow Kit. Behind him, the back side

was showing : gray hospital along the road,
a derelict kampung, green lalang

where the mud began. Sorry, he said.
I missed her so much. Then he shrugged off a wet dream,

heard pitter patter and felt damp
on his neck. Don't fucking piss on me, he cried.

*

WTC = World Trade Centre, Kuala Lumpur
Kampung = village
Lalang = grass

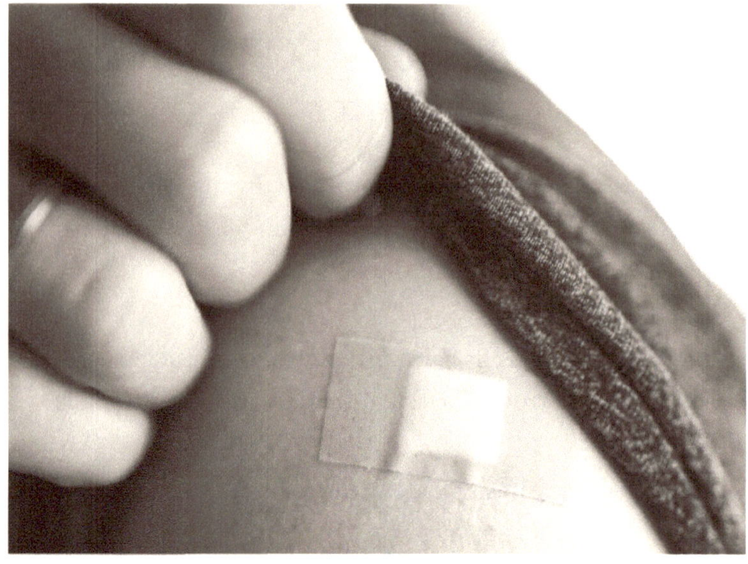

Image by Kaja Reichardt from *Unsplash*

Jab II

She held up the thing
Smiled, aimed and plunged the needle—
Prick, gritting my teeth

Let's Continue

Image by Sasikan Ulevik from *Unsplash*

Drip

(Dedicated to Air Selangor on the occasion of the water disruption of 13th - 16th October 2021)

Dd drr rri ip ip
Drip dri riii iii ip ip drip
Drip driiip drp drip

*

Air Selangor = Selangor Water

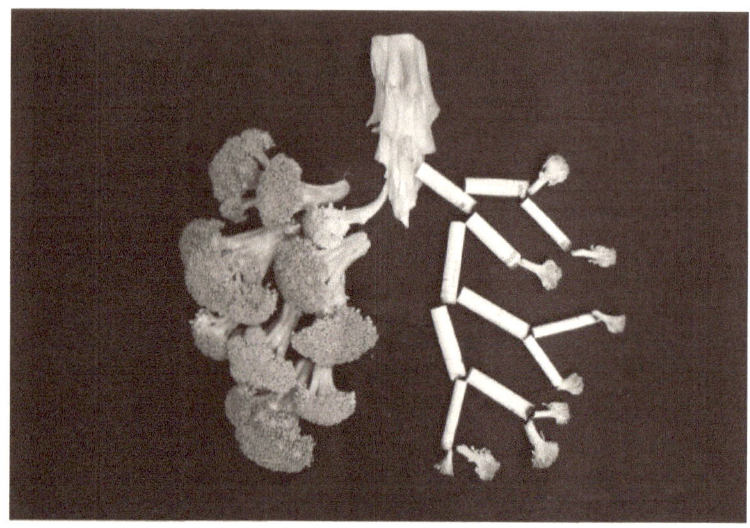

Image by Sara Bakhshi from *Unsplash*

Soaring

For Amethyst Aziezéé on the passing of her husband

When I heard
he had passed on,
my lungs heaved
liquescent, pairing
close to my alma mater.
I hadn't been aware
his December drowned,
as my New Year made
short breath of the 1st day
& raised my blood pressure,
which I figured his must
have soared even
higher, surely
to Heaven

NEW YEAR
Resolutions

Image by Tim Mossholder from *Unsplash*

New Year Resolution Without Punctuation

My new year resolutions shall not
fall short of expectations
mine not other people's
They will reach the end of the year
without a full stop because they will not keep
still
not for anyone not even for a comma
They will run their course till the year's end
leaping over obstacles like
the gaps between one's life and
the next
Oyestheywillclumptogether
formcosyintimacies
backtobackfrontandbackandfrontuponfront
all FULL frontal like the greatest
neverendingECSTASIES

Image by Jeremy Lim

Saturday night's alright

for pulled tea
but not cricking my face
at the heavens.
Behind, my chair slipped
leaned tilting tossing me abaft.
(Across, a pate sparked,
mouth curled—inverted?)
The asterisks blinked
at me dipping bouncing tumbling headlong.
No gymnast, I backflipped one-
sixth of a somersault,
smacked head, elbows, shoulders
into resisting walls kicking steps.
All sixes and sevens,
I settled—sixty-one points!
clatters the chair.
Clamped standing ovation
on the landing.

*

About this poem

"Saturday night, after the Readings, after a bunch of us, readers, attendees and organizer went for a tea break, Jeremy Chin, another writer, and I headed to this Indian eatery behind the Bangsar LRT. No idea why we sat facing the steps leading up to the forecourt, and why I had to place myself right behind them.

We chatted through the night. And then it happened. My chair slipped off the edge. Looking back, I'm astounded how I didn't come out of this with broken neck, limbs, body. Surprisingly no blood, merely bruises and a lump on my head."
—Leon Wing

pulled tea : direct translation of the Malay "teh tarik"

Image by Evie S from *Unsplash*

Feathers

Little teeny white feathers
in the room
Window closed to the outside
Door shut
I pincer a few
Throw them away?
They look so clean
Fallen from
chickens shaking water
off their backs?
Neighbors rearing birds?
They can't be keeping an
angel fallen from grace!

Image by Avinash Kumar from *Unsplash*

I'm Not Talking to My Dead Cat

It's OK, I haven't been whispering
Hey ... to my cat, past and gone,
not to the one photo I bring up
from my phone when needs must.
It's alright, though I haven't let her memory
slip from old age, even though
it's been more than fifteen months since
I left her under someone's garden,
my farewell a sodden mess of tissues and shirt sleeves.
It's always good to know at least I can ask the phone Hey ...
reassured that under the glow her smile
rubs away the soil over her face.
It's ok, even though my face is drenched,
not from the day's heat,
but from the reply to my Hey ...

Image by Alexander Grey from *Unsplash*

Sandman Cometh

damn crap about lucid dreaming when you can't pull
yourself up and when you eventually manage it and
break the surface you still haven't caught on
yet that your eyes are welling and spilling
over belying your consciousness and
your realization of having come
up from
un-
-der

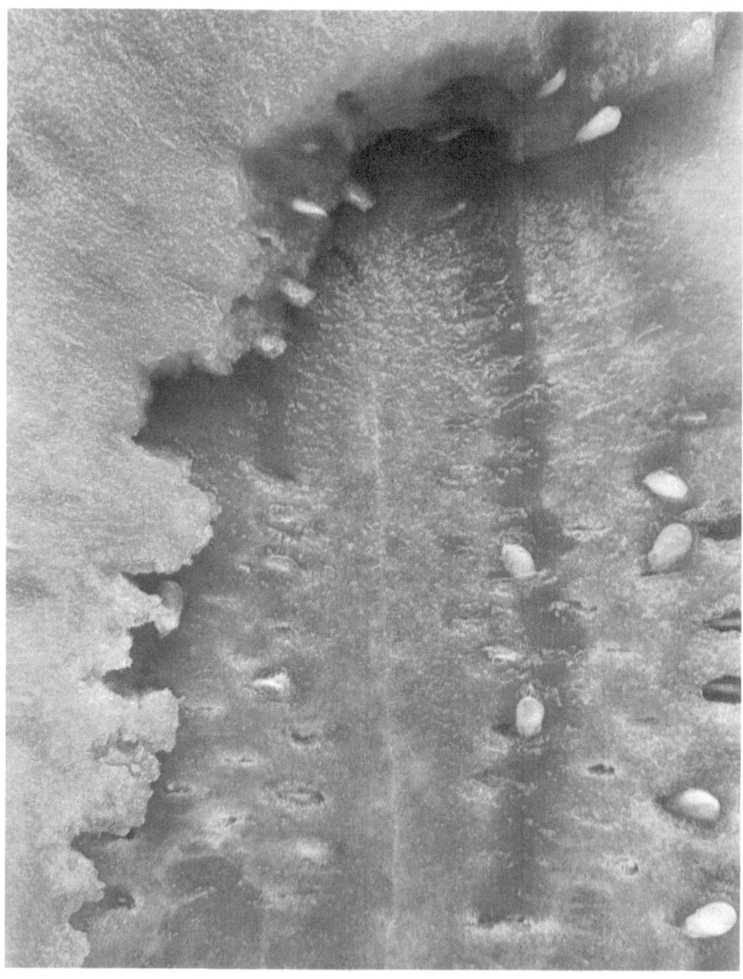

Image by Irene Kredenets from *Unsplash*

Mouthfuls

Hands weary heaving
Melons the span of a man
Who dreams of mouthfuls

Image by Anas Alhajj *Unsplash*

Gnash

Her teeth slice through gnash
The entire pomelo whole
Making space for cock

Image by Charlie Deets from *Unsplash*

Immerse

Juice sloshes the screen
cresting over gears drowning
him in ecstasy

Image by Peyton Tuttle from *Unsplash*

Die

Death is not coming
On leave till you walk back in
Waving your booty

Samples from 'Drawing Sounds'

(Bonus material only on print version)

45

Fu*k fug

It is not any blood-filled
desire of mine to go fu*k
Fu*k it I'm in this fug
Fug in the brain in the
Legs They don't cross
Each other Their inner
Thighs don't touch for
Having the legs, the feet,
Cross forward and back
Like some lovers stirring
Fu*k it Time to get this
These nates off sacks

Catspeak

Me? How
Are you looking at
Me? How?
With just one eye?
Yes, the better to look on you.
My own
Eyes I descry
On your round
lake of huge
Dark deep one.
In it my languid body
lays all rounded,
My belly all grown up,
Like I'm my own mother
Me? How?

Painting Sounds

(on 24 September 2005, at
67 Jalan Tempinis 1, Bangsar, Kuala Lumpur)
Painted piglets behind me,
Fat and flat on four wood panels,
Prod silent trotters into my back.
I poise poetic before twenty-
Odd still-life visitants in arty
Attitudes: seated, slouching, alert, standing.
The papers in my hot grip drag heavy,
Canvases with characters print-painted.
Larynx brushes stroke sonic my words,
Drawing sound colours out,
Daubing hard on plosives.
The lines waver, the paper corners flutter
In the wind of my dread
As I wax and press on ahead.

Haiku variations: Kiss

Your kiss ever shall
Stay a beautiful scar to
Last my memories

—

Your kiss forever
Bears a scar not forgotten
bruising memories

—

Your kiss forever
Bears a scar not easily
Forgotten on skin

—

Your kisses remain
as scars not so easily
abrading my skin

—

Kisses, butterflies
Landing, remaining every
Where, scarring my skin

—

Kisses: butterflies
tattooing lightly on skin
as bruises from love

Forgive

Forgive me farther,
For it has been two weeks since
My last confection
Of prose and poems,
Of which the last couple I have gone metric,
Rhyming like nobody's business.
Forgive me further, for I have seen
No light to guide my errant fingers
Back onto my keyboard,
For they have been in the grips
Of pages and pages of
Intrigue, lusts, desires, heartaches, pain,
And all manner of emotions and confrontations.
And I must gravely confess
To roving eyes over heaving
Words and writings all
Not of my doing
But of Hari Kunzru, Jane Gardam,
Nadine Gordimer, Ali Smith, and more.
Forgive me still farther
If by exactly seven days
I don't wrench my sweaty palms
Off pages by these people and their ilk,
And put fingers to key pads
For a new blog posting.
Three Hail Mary!

'Come in, will you'

Come in, will you,
into my care.
Drop the mizzle from your calico. Dry
Your shanks against my feet. Sleep is nigh,
So leap in, face down on my counterpane.
Supper's ready as soon as I sop up the pain,
The drops of cries, before I chance to realize
The fading winkling from those eyes.
Don't you care?
Come back, won't you.

Ne Fillip ne a-Larkin'

If books be the food of Reading
Its residents would Brook ne – Any - tha
nks, especially no taking the Mickey,
Trying to be Cunning, ham-
Ming it all up, Shakin' a Spear,
They being all serious when their Baker
Has not a Nickel, a son, yes.
If he has – the first one – he canne just
Fillip it a-Larkin, can he?

Don't miss out!

Visit the website below and you can sign up to receive emails whenever Leon Wing publishes a new book. There's no charge and no obligation.

https://books2read.com/r/B-A-QAEF-NZTDC

BOOKS 2 READ

Connecting independent readers to independent writers.

Did you love *Vaccy Years*? Then you should read *Drawing Sounds*[1] by Leon Wing!

[2]

The title of this collection hints at the way the poet registers the sounds in his poems as visuals. Readers will encounter poems about sex, love, lust, death, whores, evil, cakes, tablets, cats, public speaking, haikus, gym, the tsunami in Asia, ageing, tripping, clubbing, plus a few whimsical pieces--all colored by synaesthesia. The poet wrote most of them in free verse, but he didn't forget to put in a couple of rhymes in a few, to underpin the painted or drawn sounds.

Read more at wingsworldweb.tumblr.com.

---

1. https://books2read.com/u/bMry0B

2. https://books2read.com/u/bMry0B

About the Author

Leon Wing's poems can be found in PoetryPoem, Readings from Readings 2, The Malaysian Poetic Chronicles, Eksentrika, Rambutan Literary, and Haikuniverse.

A poem about the Syrian migration to Europe is featured in the Fixi anthology Little Basket 2017. He occasionally takes some poem apart and puts it back together, on the poetry blog puisipoesy.blogspot.com.

He has short stories published in Eksentrika, Queer Southeast Asia and the Canadian Asian literary magazine Ricepaper, and in anthologies like PJ Confidential and Remang, a collection of Malaysian ghost stories.

Read more at wingsworldweb.tumblr.com.

About the Publisher

Published in Malaysia by WingWorldWeb, an imprint of wingsworldweb.tumblr.com